THE BREAD, THE CUP, THE CALL AND THE CHALLENGE

THE BREAD, THE CUP, THE CALL AND THE CHALLENGE

A Maundy Thursday Drama
With Communion

BY ROGER E. LOPER

C.S.S Publishing Co., Inc.
Lima, Ohio

THE BREAD, THE CUP, THE CALL AND THE CHALLENGE

Copyright © 1992 by
The C.S.S. Publishing Company, Inc.
Lima, Ohio

You may copy the material in this publication if you are the original purchaser, for use as it was intended (worship material for worship use; educational material for classroom use; dramatic material for staging and production). No additional permission is required from the publisher for such copying by the original purchaser only. Inquiries should be addressed to: The C.S.S. Publishing Company, Inc., 628 South Main Street, Lima, Ohio 45804.

Scripture quotations are from the New Revised Standard Version of the Bible, copyright 1989 by the Division of Christian Education of the National Council of the Churches of Christ in the USA. Used by permission.

9207 / ISBN 1-55673-389-5   PRINTED IN U.S.A.

When the hour came, he took his place at the table, and the apostles with him. He said to them, "I have eagerly desired to eat this Passover with you before I suffer; for I tell you I will not eat it until it is fulfilled in the kingdom of God."
— Luke 22:14

Preface

    The play *The Bread, The Cup, The Call And The Challenge* recalls the time when the disciples ate a last meal with Jesus. It is now one year later and the disciples, this time joined by Matthias who was chosen to take the place of Judas Iscariot, meet together in the same upper room as before. They remember the events of the past year including their joys as well as their frustrations.

    Peter, who acts as the host for the meal, reminds the others to remember the call of Jesus and accept the challenge to go out and make decisions and observe all that Jesus commanded.

    The play gives not only a history of each disciple but also conveys the feeling that these men were human and faced the same temptations, discouragements and failures we might encounter if we had lived in their day.

    The play is most appropriate when used on Holy Thursday (Maundy Thursday) although it could be adapted for any communion service.

Maundy Thursday Worship

*Call To Worship

We have come here this evening, even as the disciples of Jesus came long ago, to a room to celebrate the Passover meal and to remember the last supper.

Help us to use this opportunity to examine our lives in the light of your love. We know that we have left undone things we should have done — and we have done many things we should not have done.

We need your forgiveness, God, and ask you to help us amend our lives.

Help us to follow your commandments and to walk in the footsteps of Jesus all the days of our lives.

*Opening Hymn: "O Jesus, I Have Promised"

*Psalter Reading: Psalm 116:12-19

Old Testament Reading: Jeremiah 31:31-34

Anthem or Special Music

New Testament Reading: 1 Corinthians 11:23-26

*Hymn: "What Wondrous Love Is This"

The Bread, The Cup, The Call And The Challenge

Holy Communion (by intinction)

*Hymn: "O Master, Let Me Walk with Thee"

*Benediction

Introduction

This play takes place in the upper room in Jerusalem. The year is 34 A.D., one year after Jesus met with his disciples for a last meal before his death. The time is Passover.

Matthias joins the 11 as guest of honor for the evening meal. Peter is the host for the Passover meal and along with a servant welcomes each disciple as they enter. After Peter greets each disciple the ritual handwashing is observed, the servant seeing to this responsibility. While the narrator is introducing the time and place the disciples enter, mingle, chat and share before being seated by the servant.

The seating is done around a triclinium, or three-sided reclining table. It was the custom in those days that one would recline while eating. One would rest on the left elbow and eat with the right hand. The arrangement is illustrated on page 11.

Seating Arrangement

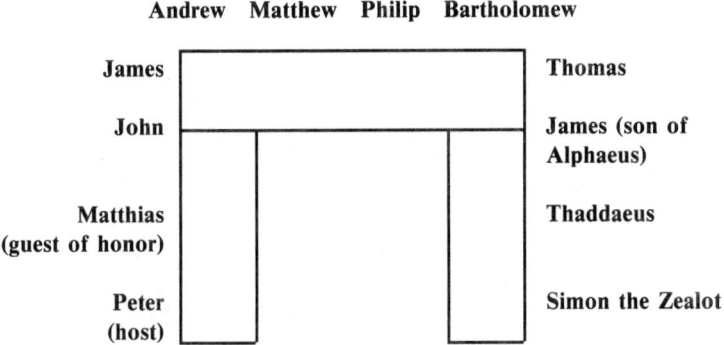

Cast of Characters

Peter (host for the meal)
Servant
Matthias
John
Bartholomew
James
Andrew
Matthew
Philip
Thomas
James (son of Alphaeus)
Thaddaeus
Simon (the Zealot)

The Bread, The Cup, The Call And The Challenge

Narrator: The year is 34 A.D.
(Peter already in with servant)

Simon: Peter, Peter.
(Simon enters)

Narrator: The day is Passover.
(Thomas enters)

Narrator: The setting is the upper room in the city of Jerusalem.
(Andrew and Matthias enter)

Narrator: One year has passed since the Passover meal, which we have come to know as the last supper.
(James and John enter)

Narrator: That Passover or last supper with Jesus was one in which he gave new meaning to the traditional bread and cup.
(Philip enters)

Narrator: Many things have happened in the lives of these disciples since they were together here in this room with Jesus.
(Bartholomew enters)

Narrator: Today the disciples have gathered together to partake of the Passover meal, reminisce about their last time with Jesus and talk about their personal experiences throughout the year.
(James [son of Alphaeus], Thaddaeus and Matthew enter)

Narrator: Listen carefully as these men share the bread, the cup, the call and the challenge.
(Each disciple is seated by the servant)

Peter: My friends, it is indeed good to be united once more around this Passover table and in this room, this room that holds many memories for each of us. We have been scattered to the east, west, north and south, proclaiming the saving message of our Lord, Jesus Christ and I commend you each for your faithful service and for continuing to carry out our Lord's commission to "make disciples, baptizing them in the name of the Father, Son and Holy Spirit." I also commend you for instructing all to observe what he has commanded.

Simon: I must confess it has not always been easy, dear brother. We were instructed to be good examples for those who scrutinize our ministry. That has been difficult, to say the least.

Thomas: Yes, I know that is true through my own experiences. Every now and then I admit I grow weary and begin entertaining selfish thoughts such as returning home. I do not feel I should be commended.

Peter: I understand these feelings, my friend. They are not foreign, even to me, but the Lord commanded us to be faithful with no promise that it would be easy. Since none of us have given up in the struggle, we have been faithful. Thus we are to be commended. Let us proceed with this blessed Passover meal. "Praised be Thou, O Lord our God, King of the Universe, who hast created the fruit of the vine. Praised be thou, O Lord, our God, King of the Universe, who causest the earth to yield food for all."
(The disciples cover their heads while Peter gives the blessing over the bread and cup.)

Andrew: Peter, my brother.

Peter: Yes, Andrew.

Andrew: Thank you for making the arrangements for this evening's meal. It is indeed good to be together again. It is also good to have Matthias, who was chosen to take the place of Judas, here with us.

Matthias: *(Craig)*

And I want to thank each of you for choosing me to be an integral part of this ministry. As one of the 70 sent by our Lord, I know the importance of this ministry. Thus I will continue to carry out my tasks in love . . . and faithfulness.

James: *(Bruce)*

It is indeed a blessing to be chosen! John, do you remember just four years ago when we were fishing with our father, Zebedee? Our Lord came right up to us and asked if we wanted to be fishers of men!

John: *(Garry)*

Yes, I do remember that, James. It seemed very strange at first. Very strange. And yet, we did not hesitate. It would have been easier to stay with the familiar, to stay on the boat with father who needed us, by the way.

James: *(Bruce)*

It would have been easy, indeed dear brother and much more practical, I must say. It was a hard life, but at least we had a steady income then!

John: *(Garry)*

Ah yes, but James, we would still be lacking in one very important thing that we do have now. That is peace of mind. We know we are doing God's will. And that is most important.

Philip: *(Ken)*

This meal is delicious, Peter. I will never forget another meal we shared together. Do you all remember? The multitude had followed us around the north rim of the lake as we were traveling by boat. They were waiting for us when we disembarked and they were hungry. I was beside myself as to how we would feed so many and where we would get enough food;

we had only five loaves and two fish? What a miracle! Jesus simply blessed those loaves, distributed the two fish and incredibly, there was more than enough for all! From that moment on I no longer doubted the power of Jesus.

Bartholomew: *Bernie* So true Philip. I am so glad that you introduced me to Jesus. But if you recall I did not believe the Messiah should come from Nazareth, that small town on the road to nowhere. Then you urged me to come and meet him in person. I will never forget the moment Jesus saw me. He recognized me immediately as the one who had been sitting under the fig tree. I wondered how he knew that? Now I know. Still wondering and doubt are things that hamper my ministry at times, I feel. I know you will keep this in your prayers, brothers. I remember prayers for one other such doubter. Isn't that right, Thomas?

Thomas: *Rob* Yes, Bartholomew. That was definitely true of me. I am so sorry I was not with you all on our Lord's first visit to this very room. But I am eternally grateful to have been here on the second occasion. I will never forget when Jesus invited me to examine the wounds in his hands, feet and side; all I could say was "my Lord and my God." That experience was so profound it nearly vanquished the word doubt from my vocabulary!

Thaddaeus: *Rick* Matthew, you have been strangely quiet up to now . . .

Matthew: *Perry* I realize I have not said anything. But it has not been out of disinterest. Rather due to an ocean of thoughts flowing through my head.

James, I can vividly relate to your feelings when you gave up the boat to follow Jesus. I, too, gave up quite a lifestyle. I had everything I could want: money, position and status. You will remember that I was a tax collector when Jesus called me. I will never forget that day. Jesus came nigh to my toll booth, he turned and said, "Come, follow me." All I could do was get up, leave everything and . . . follow! Like Zacchaeus, I gave up my entire wealth and status. I must confess my humanity. Moments of regret do crop up. The desire for wealth and nice things did not magically disappear from me at once. It was through earnest prayer, grace and support through the fellowship of believers that the Lord gave me victory over this. In return, I am truly learning how to live!

James: For each one of us, following the call of Jesus meant great risk and material loss. But I, James, the son of Alphaeus, must simply give witness to you that it was all for gain. Listen as we reflect on the call that each one of us received, we do not speak of loss but of great gain. Things that we have learned, things that we have only begun to realize and the joy we find therein. So I must assert to you that Jesus was truly God's Son, the Savior, Messiah and Redeemer of the world. You agree, don't you dear Thaddaeus?

Thaddaeus: Ah, yes. Something I will never forget of our Lord is how he said, "All a person must do is love me, keep my word and he will find favor with me and my Father." Finding that favor, dear brother, is more valuable than finest gold. May we all continue to remain faithful in our calling, till his kingdom comes.

Simon: *Barry*

At first, I, Simon the Zealot, like many had hoped that Jesus would set up an earthly kingdom and lead us in taking up the sword against our enemy Rome. But now, during this time of reflection, I see I was wrong. I failed to see his kingdom was not only here in Jerusalem, but would go to the ends of the earth. The spread of his kingdom is becoming a reality through the accomplishments of all Jesus' faithful followers. May God give us each the strength to continue and to truly go even to the ends of the earth with his message, no matter what the cost.

Peter: *Dave*

I agree that all of us have given up much at the time of our call. But, may we never be guilty of ignoring that which was gained when answering that call.

In preparing for the challenge before us, it would be fitting that before we part let us share once again the bread and the cup, remembering that time when our Lord commanded us to do this in remembrance of him.

I have asked the servant to prepare the elements, that we might share once again in that sacred act, instituted by our Lord.

Each time we break this bread and drink of this cup we proclaim the Lord's death until he comes, and in addition we reflect on the call and accept its challenges.

(The play may conclude with Peter's final speech or all the disciples could partake of the Lord's supper with Peter and the servant administering the sacrament. If the servant is an ordained minister, this would be most appropriate. An invitation to the congregation by either the servant or Peter would be in order with communion by intinction.)

Holy Communion
By Intinction

Invitation

Christ, our Lord invites to his table all who love him and who desire to live in peace and love with one another. Partake, if you are sorry for the wrongs you have done to others and God, if you intend to show more love to your family and friends, if you desire to follow the teachings of Jesus and where real meaning is given to his passion and death. If so, draw near with faith and make your humble confession to God, asking him to come into your heart and mind this day.

Participants will be invited to come and each will first take a piece of bread from the broken loaf and then dip it into the juice, partaking of both together. As the bread is taken the pastor will say:
>The Body of our Lord, broken for you.
>The Blood of Christ, given for you.

The service will close with a prayer from the pastor and a closing hymn and benediction.